FAVORITE MELODIES
THE WORLD OVER

arranged by Jane Smisor Bastien

The Bastien Older Beginner Piano Library

PREFACE

FAVORITE MELODIES THE WORLD OVER, LEVEL 1 is designed to supplement **THE OLDER BEGINNER PIANO COURSE, LEVEL 1.** However, this volume may be used as supplementary enrichment with any piano course. The timeless appeal of the well-known melodies will provide hours of enjoyment for the pianist and listener.

Published by Kjos West.
Distributed by Neil A. Kjos Music Company.
National Order Desk, 4382 Jutland Dr., San Diego, CA 92117

ISBN 0-8497-5034-2
Cover Photo: Harry Crosby/Photophile

CONTENTS

CLASSIFIED INDEX

SING ALONG FAVORITES

Give My Regards to Broadway

GEORGE M. COHAN

Reuben and Rachel

WILLIAM GOOCH

Reu-ben, Reu-ben, I've been think-ing, What a grand world this would be,

If the men were all trans-port-ed Far be-yond the North-ern Sea.

Oh my good-ness, gra-cious, Ra-chel, What a strange world this would be,

If the men were all trans-port-ed Far be-yond the North-ern Sea.

Little Brown Jug

R.A. EASTBURN

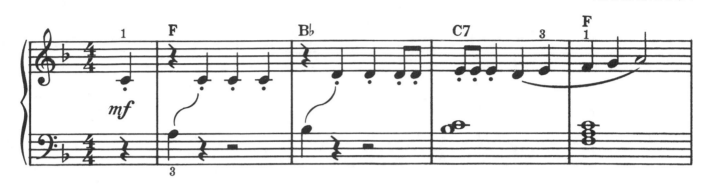

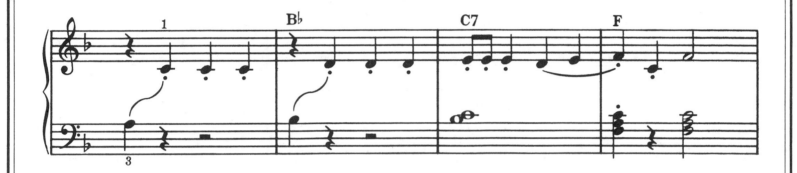

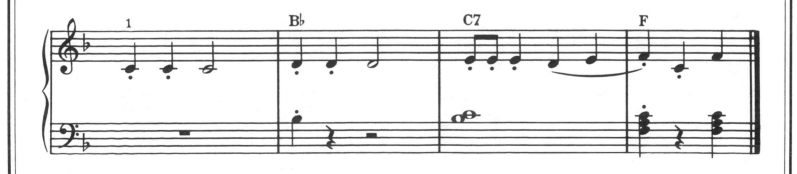

The Camptown Races

STEPHEN FOSTER

Oh, Susanna

STEPHEN FOSTER

A Bicycle Built for Two
(Daisy Bell)

HARRY DACRE

Ta-ra-ra Boom-der-e

HENRY J. SAYERS

The Sidewalks of New York

CHARLES B. LAWLOR

JAMES W. BLAKE

WP37

Heart of My Heart

ANDREW MACK

In the Good Old Summertime

RON SHIELDS

GEORGE EVANS

hold her hand and she holds yours, And that's a ver-y good sign That she's your toot-sey woot-sey In the good old sum-mer time.

In the Evening by the Moonlight

JAMES A. BLAND

Meet Me in St. Louis, Louis

ANDREW B. STERLING

KERRY MILLS

My Wild Irish Rose

CHAUNCEY OLCOTT

Old Folks at Home

STEPHEN FOSTER

Long, Long Ago

THOMAS H. BAYLY

mf Tell me the tales that to me were so dear,

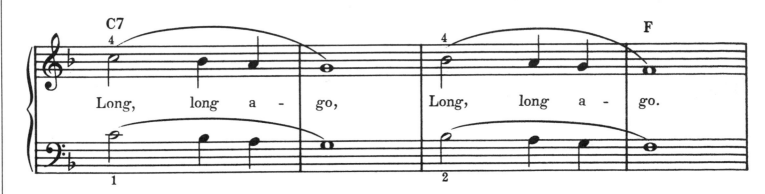

Long, long a - go, Long, long a - go.

Sing me the songs I de - light - ed to hear,

Long, long a - go, Long a - go.

Now you are here, all my grief is re - moved,

Let me for - get that so long you have roved.

Let me be - lieve that you love as you loved,

Long, long a - go, Long a - go.

Carry Me Back to Old Virginny

JAMES BLAND

31

WP37

Wait Till the Sun Shines, Nellie

ANDREW B. STERLING

HARRY VON TILZER

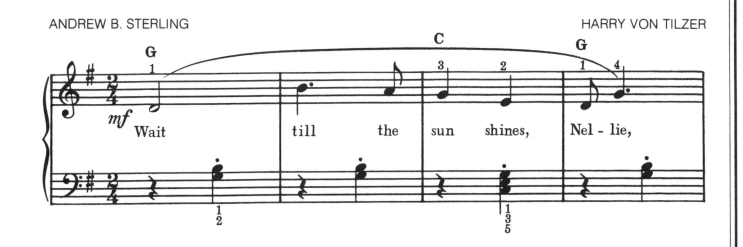

Wait till the sun shines, Nel - lie,

When the clouds go drift - ing by.

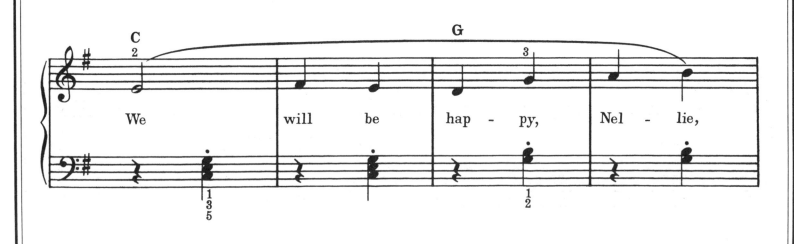

We will be hap - py, Nel - lie,

My Bonnie Lies Over the Ocean

H.J. FULMER

CHRISTMAS CAROLS

Deck the Halls

OLD WELSH AIR

mf Deck the halls with boughs of hol - ly, Fa-la-la-la-la - la - la-la-la!

'Tis the sea - son to be jol - ly, Fa-la-la-la-la - la - la-la-la!

Don we now our gay ap-par - el, Fa-la-la - la-la-la - la - la - la!

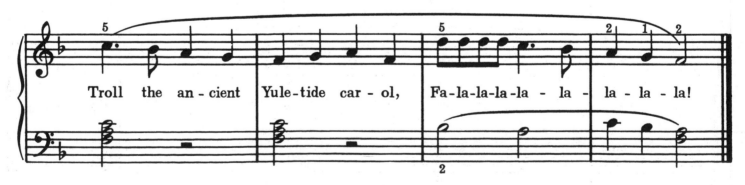

Troll the an - cient Yule-tide car - ol, Fa-la-la-la-la - la - la-la-la!

Away in a Manger

GERMAN CAROL

mp A - way in a man - ger, no crib for a bed, The

lit - tle Lord Je - sus lay down His sweet head; The

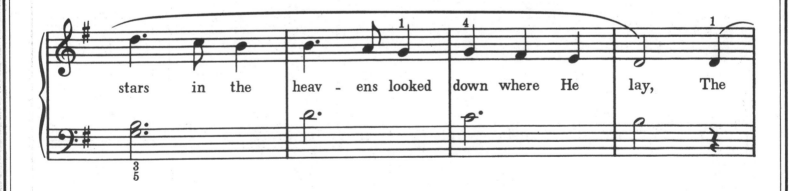

stars in the heav - ens looked down where He lay, The

lit - tle Lord Je - sus a - sleep in the hay.

Silent Night

FRANZ GRUBER

Jolly Old Saint Nicholas

TRADITIONAL

Good King Wenceslas

ENGLISH CAROL

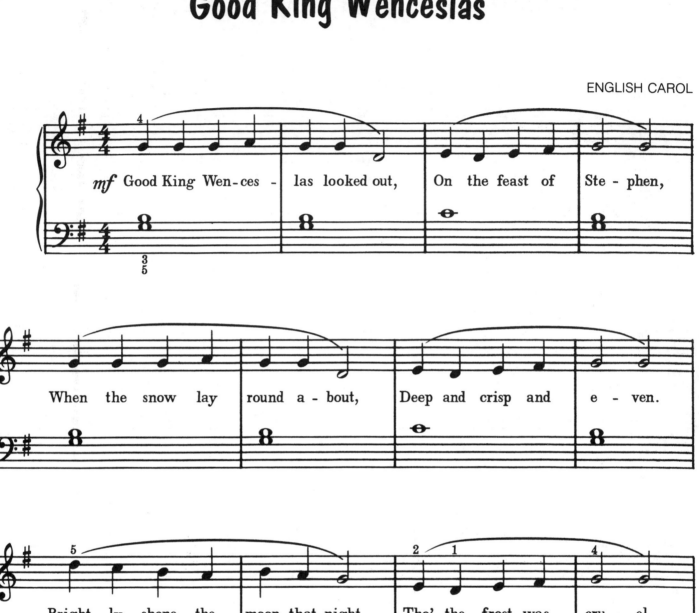

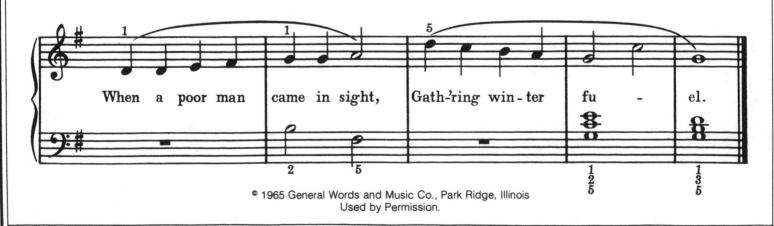

Angels We Have Heard on High

FRENCH SONG

Jingle Bells

J. PIERPONT

Up on the House-top

B.R. HANBY

The First Noel

OLD FRENCH CAROL

We Three Kings of Orient Are

JOHN H. HOPKINS

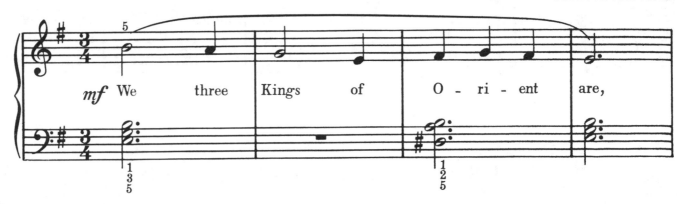

We three Kings of O - ri - ent are,

bear - ing gifts we tra - verse a - far,

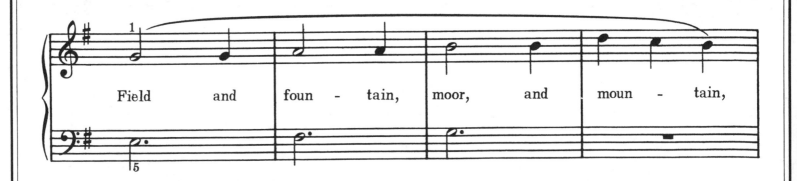

Field and foun - tain, moor, and moun - tain,

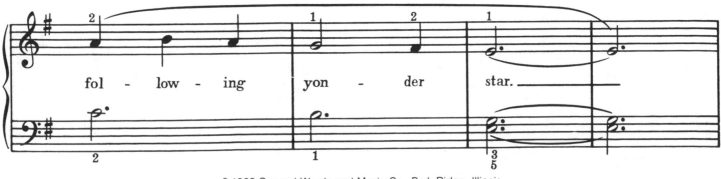

fol - low - ing yon - der star.

47

Oh,   Star of won - der, star of night,

Star with roy - al beau - ty bright,

West - ward lead - ing, still pro - ceed - ing,

Guide us to thy per - fect light.

WP37

We Wish You a Merry Christmas

ENGLISH CAROL

We wish you a Mer-ry Christ-mas, We wish you a Mer-ry Christ-mas, We

wish you a Mer-ry Christ-mas and a Hap-py New Year. Good

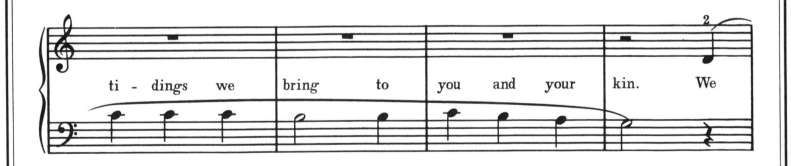

ti-dings we bring to you and your kin. We

wish you a Mer-ry Christ-mas and a Hap-py New Year.

HYMNS

Onward, Christian Soldiers

SABINE BARING-GOULD

ARTHUR S. SULLIVAN

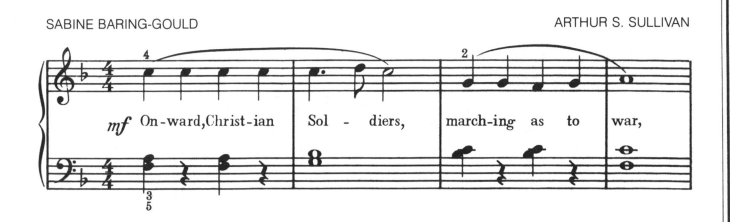

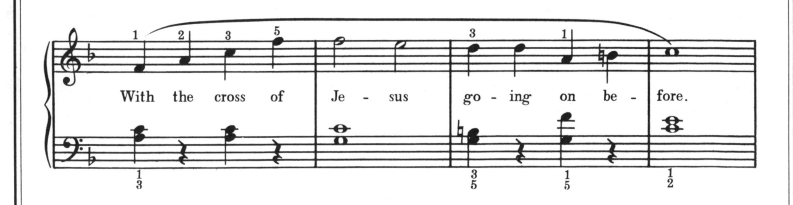

51

WP37

This Is My Father's World

MALTBIE D. BABCOCK

TRADITIONAL ENGLISH MELODY

mf This is my Fa-ther's world, And to my list-'ning ears, All na-ture sings, and round me rings The mus-ic of the spheres. This is my Fa-ther's world, I rest me in the thought Of rocks and trees, of skies and seas, His hand the won-ders wrought.

Praise God from Whom All Blessings Flow

THOMAS KEN

LOUIS BOURGEOIS

Faith of Our Fathers

FREDERICK FABER

HENRY HEMY

Rock of Ages

AUGUSTUS M. TOPLADY

THOMAS HASTINGS

mf Rock of A - ges, cleft for me, Let me hide my-self in Thee; Let the

wa - ter and the blood, From thy wound - ed side which flowed, Be of

sin the dou - ble cure, Save from wrath and make me pure.

Fairest Lord Jesus

CRUSADERS' HYMN

SILESIAN FOLK SONG

Jesus, the Very Thought of Thee

BERNARD OF CLAIRVAUX

JOHN B. DYKES

My Faith Looks Up to Thee

RAY PALMER

LOWELL MASON

mf My faith looks up to Thee, Thou Lamb of Cal - va - ry, Sav - iour Di - vine! Now hear me while I pray, Take all my guilt a - way, O let me from this day be whol - ly Thine!

We Gather Together

NETHERLANDS FOLK SONG

We gath-er to-geth-er to ask the Lord's bless-ing, He

chas-tens and has-tens His will to make known; The

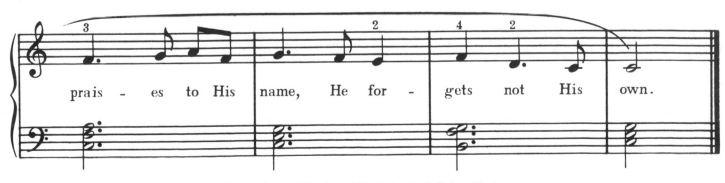

wick-ed op-press-ing cease them from dis-tress-ing, Sing

prais-es to His name, He for-gets not His own.

PATRIOTIC SONGS

The Marines' Hymn

U.S. MILITARY

The Caisson Song

EDMUND L. GRUBER

65

WP37

You're a Grand Old Flag

GEORGE M. COHAN

Ev'-ry heart beats true 'neath the Red, White and Blue, Where there's nev - er a boast or brag. But should auld ac - quaint - ance be for - got, Keep your eye on the grand old flag.

Yankee Doodle

RICHARD SHACKBURG

TRADITIONAL

When Johnny Comes Marching Home

PATRICK S. GILMORE

WP37

America the Beautiful

KATHERINE LEE BATES

SAMUEL WARD

America

SAMUEL F. SMITH

HENRY CAREY

WP37

CLASSICS

William Tell Overture

GIOACCHINO ROSSINI

"Surprise" Symphony

(Theme from 1st Movement)

JOSEPH HAYDN

Symphony No. 1

(Theme from Finale)

JOHANNES BRAHMS

Für Elise

L. VAN BEETHOVEN

WP37

La Donna E Mobile

(from "Rigoletto")

GIUSEPPI VERDI

Con spirito

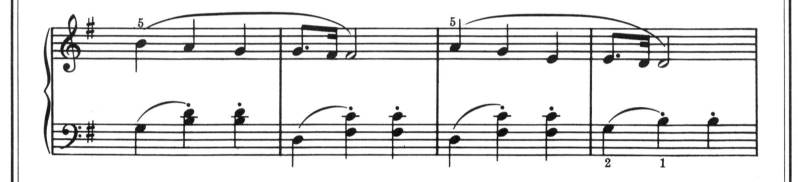

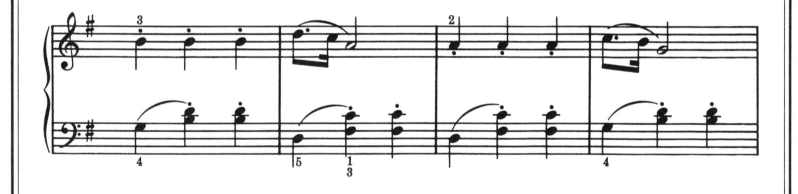

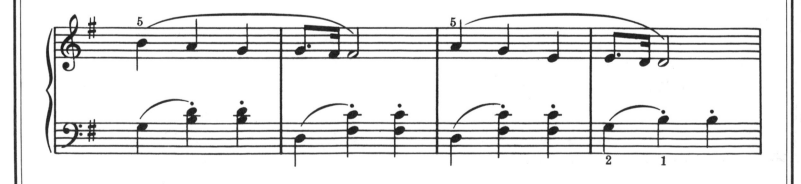

My Heart at Thy Sweet Voice

(from "Samson and Delilah")

CAMILLE SAINT-SAËNS

Slowly and expressively

Symphony No. 5

(Theme from 2nd Movement)

PETER I. TCHAIKOVSKY

Andante cantabile

WP37

Unfinished Symphony

(Theme from 1st Movement)

FRANZ SCHUBERT

Can Can

(from "Orpheus")

JACQUES OFFENBACH

Piano Concerto in A Minor

(Theme from 1st Movement)

EDVARD GRIEG

Polovetzian Dance
(from "Prince Igor")

ALEXANDER BORODIN

Pomp and Circumstance

March tempo

EDWARD ELGAR

New World Symphony

(Theme from 2nd Movement)

ANTON DVOŘÁK